LIGHTNING BOLT BOOKS™

Let's Look at Snails

Laura Hamilton Waxman

Lerner Publications Company
Minneapolis

Lerner Publications Company
A division of Lerner Publishing Group, Inc.
241 First Avenue North
Minneapolis, MN 55401 U.S.A.

Website address: www.lernerbooks.com

Library of Congress Cataloging-in-Publication Data

Waxman, Laura Hamilton.
    Let's look at snails. / by Laura Hamilton Waxman.
        p.   cm. — (Lightning bolt books™ – Animal close-ups)
    Includes index.
    ISBN 978-0-8225-7899-4 (lib. bdg. : alk. paper)
    1. Snails—Juvenile literature. I. Title.
  QL430.4.W39 2010
    594'.3—dc22   2007029226

Manufactured in the United States of America
1 2 3 4 5 6 — BP — 15 14 13 12 11 10

Contents

Snails Have Shells

Something is hiding in this shell. Can you guess what it is? Surprise! This is a snail.

This snail moves slowly along a leaf.

Snails have soft, slimy bodies.
On their backs are hard shells.

Many snails have round spiral shells. Some snails have shells that are long and pointy.

This sea snail has a spiky shell. Sea snails live in the salty ocean. Where else do snails live?

Some sea snails' shells are very colorful.

Freshwater snails live in ponds, rivers, and streams. Freshwater is not salty.

These snails live in freshwater.

Land snails live in forests, trees, and gardens. Some live on mountains or in deserts.

Snails Make Slime

This land snail is leaving behind a slimy trail. The trail is made of mucus.

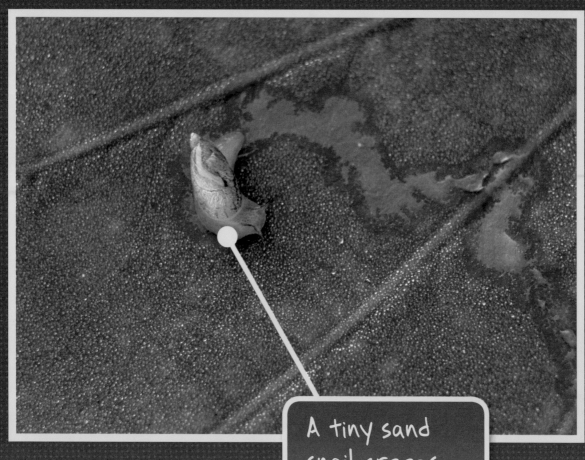

A tiny sand snail creeps across a leaf.

The mucus trail helps
the snail move.

It is like a slippery road.
The snail slides over it easily.

A snail moves along its flat bottom.

This body part looks like a belly. But it is the foot of a snail.

A snail has one flat foot that helps it move.

At the front of the foot is the head. Most land snails have four tentacles on their heads.

Can you find the snail's four tentacles?

Look closely at the ends of the two long tentacles. Do you see two black dots? These are the snail's eyes.

A snail can only see dark and light. It uses its two shorter tentacles to feel where it is going.

These snails cannot see each other well. They will use their tentacles to find their way.

A snail's mouth is near the front of its head.

Most land snails eat plants. But some snails eat animals.

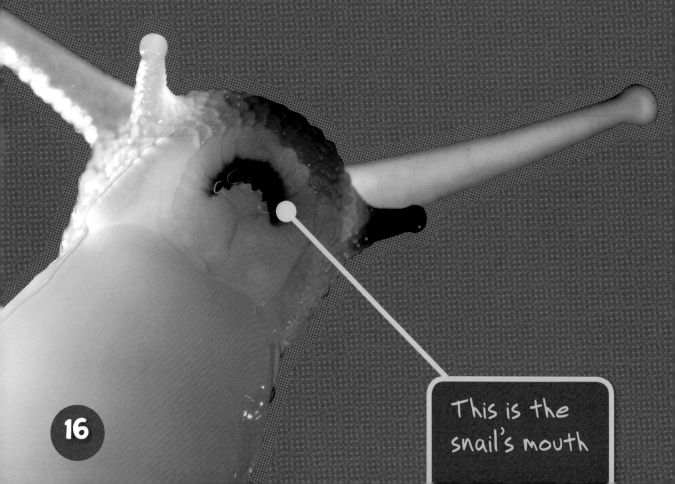

This is the snail's mouth

Snails Stay Safe

Snails look for food in damp, dark places. They try to stay out of dry, sunny places. Do you know why?

A snail will die if its body gets too dry. It can go inside its shell to stay cool and moist.

These sea snails stay safe inside their shells.

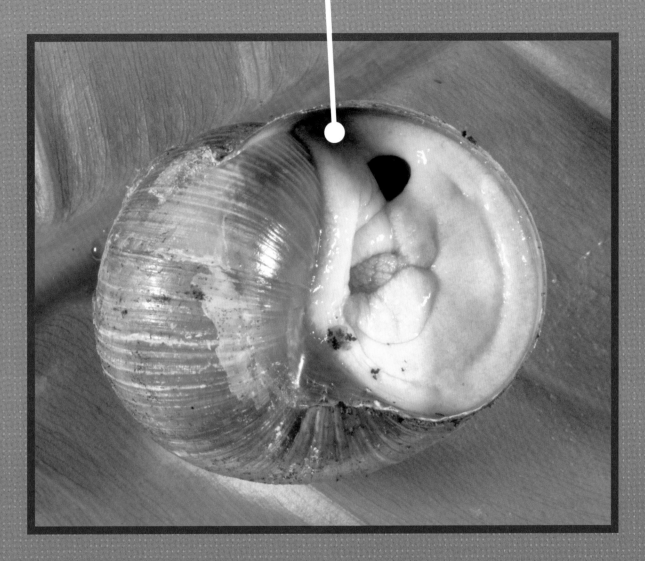

This garden snail is ready to hibernate

Some land snails hibernate in the cold winter months. The snails go into a deep sleep. Mucus seals their shells shut.

Are these snails hibernating?

No! They are hiding
from a predator.

Predators are animals that hunt and eat other animals. Many predators like to eat snails.

Hedgehogs eat snails.

Snails Lay Eggs

This snail is laying eggs in a hole in the ground. Snails hide their eggs from predators.

Inside the eggs are baby snails.
What happens to the eggs?

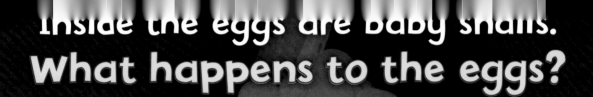

These snail
eggs are hidden
in a leaf.

The eggs hatch.
Out come tiny snails.

This tiny snail just hatched!

Baby snails are hungry. First, they eat their eggshells. Then they look for tasty plants.

A young snail eats and eats.
It grows bigger and bigger.
Its shell grows too.

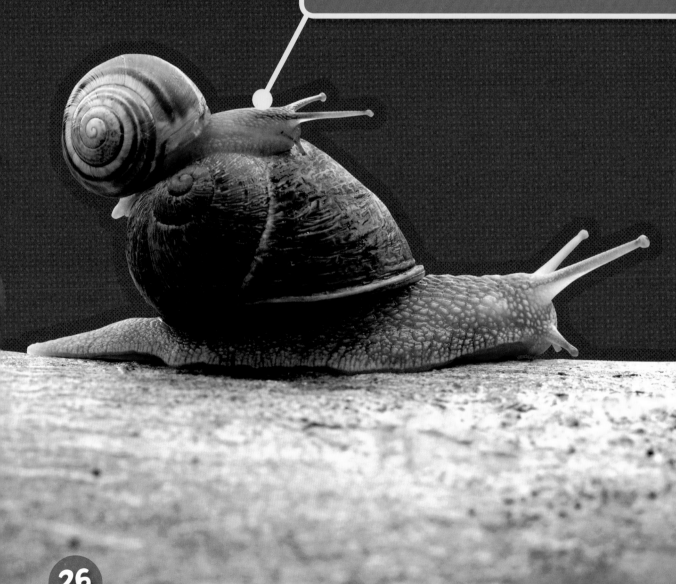

A young snail hitches a ride on its parent's back.

This slimy snail is all grown up.

27

Fun Facts

- Snails live all over the world. They come in all sizes. One of the largest snails can be found in East Africa.

- Some snails can live to be twenty years old.

- Snails that live on land tend to chew their food loudly. If you are near a large land snail, you may be able to hear it crunching and munching away!

- Snail racing is a popular pastime in some parts of Great Britain.

Snail Diagram

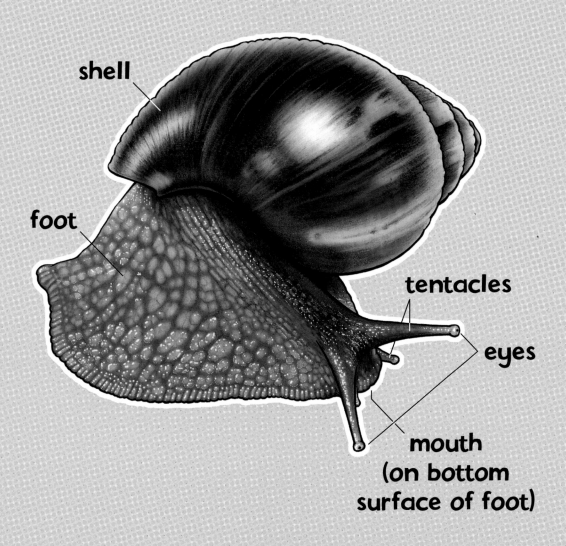

shell

foot

tentacles

eyes

mouth
(on bottom
surface of foot)

Glossary

freshwater: water that is not salty

hibernate: to go into a deep, sleeplike state

mucus: a slimy liquid. Some snails leave behind mucus trails when they move.

predator: an animal that hunts and eats other animals

spiral: a curving shape that circles around and around

tentacle: one of the long, flexible limbs on the heads of most land snails

Further Reading

All about Snails
http://www.geocities.com/sseagraves/allaboutsnails.htm

Allen, Judy. *Are You a Snail?* New York: Kingfisher, 2000.

Llewellyn, Claire. *Slugs and Snails.* New York: Franklin Watts, 2001.

Murray, Peter. *Snails.* Chanhassen, MN: Child's World, 2007.

Snails for Kids and Teachers
http://www.kiddyhouse.com/Snails

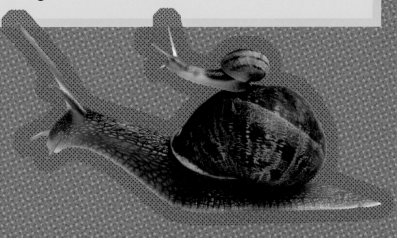

Index

Photo Acknowledgments

The images in this book are used with the permission of: © iStockphoto.com/Nicholas Homrich, p. 1; © iStockphoto.com/Chen Chih-Wen, p. 2; © Steve Winter/National Geographic/Getty Images, p. 4; © age fotostock/SuperStock, pp. 5, 11, 12, 13, 20; © Ray Coleman/Visuals Unlimited, Inc., p. 6; © Brandon Cole Marine Photography/Alamy, p. 7; © Willem Kolvoort/naturepl.com, p. 8; © Jane Burton/naturepl.com, p. 9; © Gerry Bishop/Visuals Unlimited, Inc., p. 10; © Jeff Foott/Discovery Channel Images/Getty Images, p. 14; © Justmarika/Dreamstime.com, p. 15; © Francesco Tomasinelli/Photo Researchers, Inc., pp. 16, 19; © Chris O'Reilly/naturepl.com, p. 17; © Floris Leeuwenberg/The Cover Story/CORBIS, p. 18; © Dietmar Nill/naturepl.com, p. 21; © Klaus Echle/naturepl.com, p. 22; © Inga Spence/Visuals Unlimited/Getty Images, p. 23; © Dwight Kuhn, pp. 24, 25; © Simon Battensby/Photographer's Choice/Getty Images, p. 26; © Photodisc/Getty Images, p. 27; © Pdtnc/Dreamstime.com, p. 28; © Laura Westlund/Independent Picture Service, p. 29; © Goruppa/Dreamstime.com, p. 30; © iStockphoto.com/mammamaart, p. 31.

Front cover: © Cyril Ruoso/Minden Pictures; © Martin Poole/Digital Vision/Getty Images (background).